A Jubilant So...

10 Solos by John Leavitt

❖ MEDIUM LOW VOICE ❖

ISBN 0-634-01785-3

HAL•LEONARD®
CORPORATION
7777 W. BLUEMOUND RD. P.O. BOX 13819 MILWAUKEE, WI 53213

Visit Hal Leonard Online at
www.halleonard.com

A Jubilant Song

WALT WHITMAN
From LEAVES OF GRASS

JOHN LEAVITT

Stately (♩ = 76)

Optional spoken introduction: Singers to come, musicians to come, poets, orators, singers, musicians to come,

You, a new breed, native, athletic, continental,

greater than ever before!

Arouse!

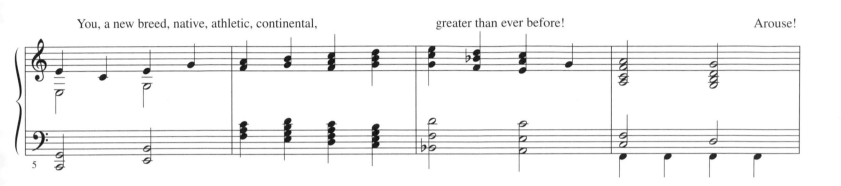

Arouse!

Brightly (♩ = 138)

Make— a song— the most jub -

Measures 1–10 are optional introduction.

-i - lant song,___ make__ a song__ full of mu - sic!

Make__ a song__ the most jub - i - lant song,___ Sing a song of___

joy!

mf

The joy of our spir - it is un - caged._____ The

Make— a song— the most jub - i - lant song!—

dim. e rit.

Ped.

Slower, with freedom (♩ = 76)

Give me to hold all sounds,— fill me with sweet mus - ic,

Give to me to hold all sounds,— fill me with sweet mus -

Brightly (♩ = 138)

ic!

Make__ a song__ the most jub - i - lant song,___ make__ a song__ full of

mu - sic! Make__ a song__ the most jub - i - lant song,___ Sing__ a song__ of__

joy!_____ Joy!

Joy!_____

A Girl's Garden

ROBERT FROST

JOHN LEAVITT

spring   When she was a girl on the farm, she

did a child - like thing. One day she ask'd her fath - er To

give her a gar - den plot To plant and tend and reap her - self, And

he said, "Why not?"

12

farm, And give you a chance to put some strength— On your slim-jim

arm."

It was not e - nough of a

And hid from an - y - one pass - ing. And then she begged the

seed. She says she thinks she plant - ed one Of all_____ things but

weed. A hill each of po - ta - toes, Rad - ish - es, let - tuce,

peas, To - ma - toes, beets, beans, pump - kins, corn, And e - ven fruit trees.

And yes, she has long mis - trust - ed That a

ci - der ap - ple tree In bear - ing there to - day is hers,

Or at least may be. Her crop was a mis - cel - la - ny When

all was said and done, A lit - tle bit of

ev - 'ry - thing,_____

dim.

A great deal of

p

p

none.

mp *poco a poco cresc.*

122

sfz *p* *cresc.*   *f*

Now _____ when she sees in the

f

126

vil - lage   How   vil - lage   things _____ go,   Just

opt.

129

when   it   seems   to   come   in   right,   She   says,   "I   know!   It's   as

rit.   *p*

rit.

132

Aura Lee

W. W. FOSDICK

GEORGE R. POULTON
Arranged by JOHN LEAVITT

1. As the black - bird in the spring, 'neath the wil - low
2. In your blush the rose was born; Mus - ic when you

tree
spoke.
Sat and piped I heard him sing,
Through your a - zure eyes the moon

Sing of Au - ra Lee,
Spark - ling seemed to break.
Au - ra Lee,

The Bells

EDGAR ALLAN POE

JOHN LEAVITT

Crisp with excitement! (♩ = *ca.* 148-152)

Hear the sledg-es with the bells — Sil - ver bells, sil - ver bells! What a world of mer - ri - ment their

mel - o - dy fore-tells!

How they tin - kle, tin - kle, tin - kle, In the ic - y air of night! While the

stars that o - ver sprin - kle All the heav - ens, seem to twin - kle With a crys - tal - line de - light, with a

crys - tal - line de - light;_____ Keep - ing

time, time, time, In a sort of Run - ic rhyme, keep - ing time, time, time, In a

Hear the sledg-es with the bells — Sil-ver bells, sil-ver bells! What a world of mer-ri-ment their

mel-o-dy fore-tells!

From the jing-ling and the tink-ling, from the jing-ling and the tink-ling of the

bells, bells! bells, bells!

8vb

Between Two Hills

CARL SANDBURG

JOHN LEAVITT

Deep River

Based on Joshua 3

African-American Spiritual
Arranged by JOHN LEAVITT

O Captain! My Captain!

WALT WHITMAN

JOHN LEAVITT

ves - sel grim and dar - ing;——— But O   heart! heart! heart!   O the bleed-ing drops of red,   Where

on the deck my Cap - tain lies,   Fall - en cold and   dead.

Cap - tain!⸺ dear fath - er!⸺ This arm be-neath your head! It

is some dream that on the deck, You've fall - en cold and dead.

meno mosso, espressivo

My Cap - tain does not an - swer, his

lips are pale and still, My fath - er does not feel my arm, he has no pulse nor will, The

the/sky/was

e. e. cummings
From TULIPS & CHIMNEYS

JOHN LEAVITT

Prairie Waters by Night

CARL SANDBURG

JOHN LEAVITT

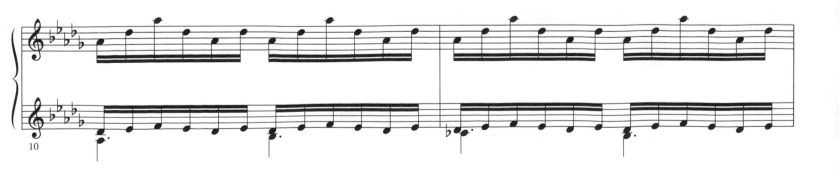

And the long wil-lows— drowse— on the shoul-ders of run-ning wa - ter, and sleep from much mu - sic; join - ed songs of day - end,

feath - er - y throats___ and ston - y

wat - ers, in___ a choir___ chant - ing

new psalms. It is too

much for the long wil - lows when low laugh - ter___

Southern Ships and Settlers

STEPHEN and ROSEMARY VINCENT BENÉT
From A BOOK OF AMERICANS

JOHN LEAVITT

Sea Chantey ($\dot{}$ = *ca.* 60)

Both Cath - 'lic and Pro - test - ant there may find

dim. *mp*

har - bor, Though I am a Cath - 'lic by creed and by prayer. The

mf

South is Vir - gin - ia, the North is New Eng - land. I'll go in the

mid - dle and plant my folk there.

f

We're the

cresc.

barques and the sail - ors, the bread on the wat - ers, The— seed that was

plant - ed and grew to be tall, And the South was first won by our

toils and our dan - gers, So re - mem - ber our jour - neys. Re - mem - ber us

all.

In South Car-o-li-na, the cock-fight-ing plant-ers Will dance with their belles by a trop-i-cal star. In North Car-o-li-na, the stur-dy Scotch I-rish Will prove at King's Moun-tain the met-al they are.

Unhurried, with freedom

I'll set - tle them pleas - ant - ly on the Sa - van - nah, With

Ger - mans and High - land - ers, thrift - y and strong, They'll eat Geor - gia

peach - es in huts of pal - met - to, Their land shall be fer - tile, their

124

Tempo I

days shall be long.

129

We're the barques and the sail - ors, the

135

bread on the wat - ers, The— seed that was plant - ed and grew to be

140

tall, And the South was first won by our toils and our dan - gers, So re -

rall. *cresc.* **ff** *a tempo*

mem - ber our jour - neys. Re - mem - ber us all.

rall. *cresc.* **ff** *a tempo*

Ah!

Ped.

Dr. John Leavitt is one of the energetic young faces on the music scene. During the past 15 years he has served as a clinician or conductor for hundreds of concerts, festivals, and workshops throughout North America. He has won a decade of consecutive ASCAP annual awards for his compositions and arrangements, and his music has been performed across the globe in over 30 countries.

A native of Kansas, Dr. Leavitt was born and raised in Leavenworth. In 1990 he completed doctoral work in conducting at the University of Missouri-Kansas City Conservatory of Music. Dr. Leavitt also holds a master of music degree from Wichita State University (KS) in piano performance with additional emphasis in composition. His undergraduate work is in music education from Emporia State University (KS).

During and following the completion of his doctorate, Dr. Leavitt served as a faculty member in the music department at Friends University (KS), where he received the faculty award for teaching excellence.

Currently, Dr. Leavitt spends his time composing, conducting, and guest lecturing. In Wichita he serves as artistic director and conductor of the professionally-trained vocal ensembles known as The Master Arts Chorale and Youth Chorale, which he founded in 1990. The Master Arts Youth Chorale, under his direction, has been featured in performance in Carnegie Hall, St. Patrick's Cathedral and NBC's "Today Show." The Master Arts Adult Chorale will premier his "Requiem" in Carnegie Hall in June of 2000. He also serves as Cantor (directs the parish music program) at Reformation Lutheran Church in Wichita, Kansas.

Dr. John Leavitt